PERSONALITY LANGUAGE™

How To PERSUADE And INFLUENCE Virtually ANYONE ANYTIME

Marilyne Woodsmall, Ph. M.
&
Wyatt Woodsmall, Ph. D.

A Selection of Other Works by
Marilyne Woodsmall & Wyatt Woodsmall

The Future of Learning: The Michel Thomas Method
Freeing Minds One Person at a Time
www.thefutureoflearning.com
www.themichelthomasmethod.com

People Pattern™ Power:
The Nine Keys to Business Success
www.peoplepatternpower.com

The People Pattern™ Prayers:
What You've Always Wanted, But Were Afraid To Ask For
www.thescienceofidiots.com

Red Alert: The Culture Crisis -
Implications of the General Developmental Model

Learning How to Learn™:
Cultivating our Children for the Future

Motive: The Secret Key to Influence

The Secrets to Motivation in the Workplace

Behavioral Assessment Tools:
Profiling Plus™ - Hiring Right
The Value Culture™ Profile
The People Pattern™ Profile
The Entrecode™ Profile

PERSONALITY LANGUAGE™

How To PERSUADE And INFLUENCE Virtually ANYONE ANYTIME

Marilyne Woodsmall, Ph. M.
&
Wyatt Woodsmall, Ph. D.

Next Step Press

DEDICATION

We dedicate this book to raising awareness of the
true nature of human interaction that goes far beyond gender,
race, nationality, and creed. Our goal is to help people to discover
the secrets of enhancing their communication for success in business and
in their personal lives, and to do so with integrity and honor.
We also dedicate this book to dear Master Poufy.

CONTENTS

Forward

You are about to learn a powerful tool for human change. There is an aspect relating to the knowledge which you are about to acquire which cannot be ignored. This information is incredibly powerful to influence and to persuade others. There is a huge responsibility that comes with mastering this information, for you will have the power to change your own behavior and influence that of others in a positive way.

With this powerful knowledge and mastery of this tool for human change, comes the responsibility to use this knowledge wisely, with integrity, and in an ethical manner. As such, we expect all those who read this book to pledge the following from the very start:

THE *PEOPLE PATTERN*™ *PLEDGE*

I believe in the power of **People Patterns**™ and of **Personality Language**™. I also realize that with power comes responsibility. I promise to use my knowledge and skills with **People Patterns**™ and **Personality Language**™ in an ethical and professional manner. I will never use them to intentionally exploit or to intentionally manipulate another person in any way.

I will use my knowledge of **People Patterns**™ and of **Personality Language**™ to achieve a win/win in my daily interactions with everyone. I will also use my knowledge of **People Patterns**™ and of **Personality Language**™ to enhance communication with others and to understand and to enter into their models of the world, which may be different from my own. I will use my knowledge of **People Patterns** and of **Personality Language**™ to establish bridges of mutual understanding and positive communication.

Finally, I will use **People Patterns**™ and **Personality Language**™ with integrity and honor and wisdom in all of my interactions with my fellow men and women, in both my work and in my personal life. This I so pledge.

YOUR NAME:_____ DATE:___/___/_____

Introduction

How many times have you entered an important meeting anxiously wondering how you were going to get others to agree with your point of view? How often have you found yourself ready to address a group at a conference or at your office and were still not sure how to influence those in attendance in a positive manner? How about making a good impression with someone whom you are meeting for the first time? Given the challenges of today's economic realities, it is all the more vital to be able to communicate your message rapidly, clearly, effectively and in a way that is contextually meaningful to the person or people with whom you are doing business.

Whether you are in sales or management or in any aspect of business, it is all the more essential to have a practical and powerful new set of tools to increase your business profits as well as keep your present customers and clients no matter what the economic climate.

Wouldn't it be really helpful and useful to have a quick and immediate way of enhancing your communication with others in the business world and at the same time be able to persuade and influence them to take action in a particular situation? How about in personal relationships? Now you are about to learn the keys to positive influence. These keys are called **People Patterns™**. Many of you have heard about so-called "body language." With People Patterns™ we are dealing with an even deeper level of communication which we refer to as **Personality Language™**.

Just as you would translate a foreign language in order to communicate with someone who does not speak your native tongue, the same applies to communicating with someone who does not share your People Patterns™ or Personality Language™. This introductory book reveals the patterns and their particular components which comprise our powerful Personality Language™.

Furthermore, the ability to persuade and influence others is based on one very important secret. That secret has to do with one very significant element: structure, in particular the structure of another person's thinking. Most people focus on what they are

3

saying rather than on how they are saying it. People Patterns™ focus on the structure of people's thinking rather than the content.

Interestingly, it is not what you think you are communicating that matters. Instead, it is what the other person perceives you as saying or communicating that matters. Just as body language communicates on a subconscious level, so does what we call "Personality Language"™. In successful communication and persuasion, you have to be able to present your position and ideas in a way that makes sense to the other person or people. You have to be able to speak in the particular Personality Language™ that corresponds to that of the person or people with whom you are engaged in a given communication exchange.

In order to do this, you need to understand a powerful, fundamental truth about human behavior. It is that human beings are creatures of habit and behave in predictable ways. These so-called habits take the form of particular patterns in the various aspects of our lives: in thinking, working, eating, talking, etc. These patterns are the basis of our Personality Language™ and may or may not change contextually. Furthermore, humans display a wide range of habits or patterns that include not only the physical realm, but the mental and emotional realms as well. It is this group of mental patterns or People Patterns™, i.e. Personality Language™, which provides the keys to persuasion and enhanced communication.

People Patterns™ are specific patterns of human behavior. They are perceptual filters that are part of what we refer to as one's personal "model of the world." Although we all live in same world, each of us has our own unique set of perceptual filters that are the basis of our Personality Language™. It is through this Personality Language™ or set of People Patterns™ that we interact in the world and through which we experience people, things and events in the world. Each People Pattern™ brings certain aspects of our environment into focus while deleting or distorting other aspects. The result is that people pay attention to different things, operating out of their own respective "model of the world." There are ways to detect these People Patterns™ in ourselves and in others from observing behavior and language.

INTRODUCTION

We recommend that you begin by identifying your own People Patterns™. In fact, in reading this book you will quickly discover the triggers of your daily interactions with others in your professional and personal relationships, both past and present. You will be amazed to realize why you get along with some people and why you simply don't connect or have never been able to connect with others. You will realize why you have always thought of them as idiots or why you may have thought of yourself as an idiot at times because you felt out of place with others who were not like you and did not behave like you. With this book you will gain a new and enlightened perspective on your own behavior and that of your friends, your family, your colleagues and everyone you meet. The situations which you have experienced and the relationships that you have had or now have will suddenly make sense to you.

We are providing you with a powerful blueprint for personal growth and for growing your business by increasing your influence and ability to persuade others to take the action you would like. The way to do this is to begin to recognize these patterns in your daily life, whether at work, at home or wherever you interact with others through observation of yourself and those around you.

In **The People Pattern™ Creed,** we summarize the basic elements involved:

THE PEOPLE PATTERN™ CREED

All human beings are creatures of habit.

These habits lead to consistent patterns of behavior.

These patterns are called People Patterns™.

All of our language and our actions reflect these People Patterns™.

People Patterns™ are readily detectable by a trained observer.

People Patterns™ can be utilized to enhance communication.

People Patterns™ can also be used to increase influence.

A wise person will use them to do so.

To do anything else is to fail to respect another person's uniqueness.

In order to use the People Patterns™ effectively to influence and persuade others, whether in sales or management, or in any business context, you must be willing to change how you are doing things. In this way, you can enter another person's "model of the world" and, thus, change the way in which he or she is doing things. To accomplish this, you must be able to tailor your communication to the way in which the other person thinks and behaves. It all boils down to your ability to match the other person's People Patterns™. Once you do this, you will greatly enhance your ability to connect with other people and to influence their thinking in a positive manner.

THE OVERVIEW

To effectively match another person's People Patterns™, you need to be able to do the following things:

1. Know the outcome that you desire in your communication or interaction with that person.
2. Sharpen your sensory awareness to be able to detect the patterns reflected in a person's behavior and language.
3. Adopt flexibility of behavior so that you can change when necessary.

THE STRUCTURE

Now that you have a brief overview of People Patterns™, we would like to provide you with a quick, at-a-glance, user-friendly guide to identifying and to applying these patterns in the context of your daily business activities. The structure of this guide is such that the following information will be provided:

1. NAME of the People Pattern™

2. DESCRIPTION of the various ELEMENTS of the People Pattern™: the general behavioral characteristics of a person of this type and how to recognize them

3. POPULATION DISTRIBUTION indicates the statistical distribution of the types among the population.

4. TARGET INDICATOR QUESTIONS: Designed to enable you to quickly and easily identify the People Patterns™

5. IDENTIFICATION: How to identify the types based on answers to the **TARGET INDICATOR QUESTIONS**

6. EXAMPLES: Sample answers given to the **TARGET INDICATOR QUESTIONS** that correspond to the various components of each People Pattern™

7. UTILIZATION GUIDE: Explains what one needs to communicate with and influence a person with a particular pattern in the context of sales and management

8. LANGUAGE TO INFLUENCE: Specific words and phrases that are effective in influencing a person who operates from a particular People Pattern™.

What we are providing for you here is a Quick Reference Guide or Primer to using and to applying People Patterns™ and thus, the Personality Language™ that is context and relevance specific. This knowledge will prove to be quite useful in situations that may arise both in the workplace and in your personal life. These are all situations where effective and targeted, customized communication will make the difference between success and failure in your interactions with others.

Although this book is a comprehensive introduction to our powerful Personality Language™ Program, it is nevertheless an introduction. There are so many more refinements awaiting you in all aspects of your life and work. And there is so much more to discover about your own set of People Patterns™ that are the basis of your Personality Language™ and those of your associates, family members and anyone you meet.

PERSONALITY LANGUAGE™

Chapter I

THE MOTIVATION PEOPLE PATTERN™

How people motivate themselves to do anything in life

Types:

A. Move Toward

B. Move Away From

There are two basic reasons why anyone ever does anything in life: for carrots or for sticks. They are either **move toward** or **move away from** in orientation, respectively. These are the two aspects of the **Motivation People Pattern™**.

DESCRIPTION

MOVE TOWARD

Move toward people do things because they want to accomplish certain goals, achieve outcomes or want to attain certain things.

MOVE TOWARD People:

1. Set priorities
2. Are good at managing priorities
3. Have difficulty in recognizing what should be avoided
4. Are often oblivious to what is not working or to what is going awry
5. Respond best to incentives, i.e., carrots

MOVE AWAY FROM

Move away from people do things because they want to avoid certain situations, things or people.

MOVE AWAY FROM People:

1. Are motivated to steer clear of, avoid or eliminate situations, things, etc.
2. Have difficulty managing priorities
3. Have trouble maintaining focus of goals
4. Are easily distracted by negative situations or things
5. Respond best to threats, i.e., sticks

POPULATION DISTRIBUTION

Move Toward: 50%

Move Away From: 50%

TARGET INDICATOR QUESTIONS

What do you want in a job?

What do you want in a car?

GENERAL PATTERN: What do you want in a_____?

IDENTIFICATION

Move Toward People

1. Talk about what they want
2. Tell you what they will achieve, accomplish, obtain, get, gain, attain or have
3. Talk about people, things and situations that they want to include

Move Away From People

1. Talk about what they don't want
2. Tell you what they will avoid or steer away from, get rid of or be repulsed by
3. Talk about people, things and situations that they want to exclude

EXAMPLES

Move Toward

1. I want a job that pays well, is exciting and has growth potential.
2. I want a car that is classy and sleek.
3. I want a bank that provides excellent customer service.

Move Away From

1. I don't want a job in which the boss is always looking over my shoulder.
2. I don't want a car that is always breaking down and that gets bad gas mileage.
3. I don't want a bank that is always pestering me or where there are unpleasant tellers.

UTILIZATION GUIDE

SALES

Move Toward:

1. Present or package your product or service so as to emphasize what the product or service will do for the customer or client.
2. Move Toward people will want to know how the product or service will help them.
3. Emphasize the benefits of your product or service.

4. Show how your product or service will meet the customer's needs.

5. Talk about features that give your customers what they want.

Move Away From:

1. Stress how your product or service will help them to avoid things or issues that they don't want.

2. Emphasize how it will help your client or customer to minimize problems and hassles.

3. Make sure that you sell them a maintenance contract.

4. Stress how your product or service does not have drawbacks that other products have (that they have used).

5. Provide a guarantee if possible.

MANAGEMENT

Move Toward:

1. Offer carrots: bonuses and incentives and other employment perks.

2. Stress goals and what employees can get, attain, achieve and accomplish.

3. Be aware that they may be blind to or ignore potential problems.

4. Don't expect them to respond to threats and punishment.

Move Away From:

1. Use sticks: threats, sanctions and punishment.

2. Make certain that the threats and sanctions are real and believable.

3. In group discussion, it is vital to be able to control their tendency to always bring up problems.

4. Don't expect them to respond to incentives.

LANGUAGE TO INFLUENCE

Move Toward

Get, attain, attract, achieve, accomplish, include, have, obtain.

Move Away From

Avoid, annoyed by, repulsed by, get rid of, eliminate, do away with, not have, exclude, steer clear of, eradicate, remove, keep away from.

Chapter II

THE CHANGE PEOPLE PATTERN™

How people deal with change

Types:

A. Sameness

- Qualified Sameness

B. Difference

- Qualified Difference

The Change People Pattern™ reflects the manner in which an individual perceives the world. In any given situation, individuals will focus their attention on or will notice one of two things: *sameness* or *difference*. A Sameness orientation looks for commonalities while a Difference orientation makes distinctions.

The particular choice of pattern will directly influence how a person will deal with change in his or her life, as well as the degree to which the person will tolerate any change. The Change People Pattern™ has a direct correlation with how long a person will remain in a given job. It will also reflect a specific lifestyle that is either geared to one's world staying the same, or changing all the time, or else changing intermittently, to varying degrees, as we shall see.

DESCRIPTION

SAMENESS

Sameness people will focus their attention on things that are similar or the same, or on elements that match things which they have previously experienced in one way or another.

SAMENESS People:

1. Do not tolerate change
2. Desire the *status quo*
3. Are quite uncomfortable with things that are different from their experiences
4. Can remain in a job from 15 years to life without variety
5. Prefer continuity of lifestyle both personally and professionally
6. In a job, require repetition of task

QUALIFIED SAMENESS

Qualified Sameness people will first notice similarities and then differences in a given situation or experience.

QUALIFIED SAMENESS People:

1. Like things to remain basically the same with occasional variety
2. Prefer change to occur gradually and slowly
3. Want a job that evolves little by little over a period of time
4. Tend to stay in their jobs from 7 to 9 years
5. Represent the average business person
6. Desire improved versions of what they already have

DIFFERENCE

Difference people will always focus on what is different in a given situation or notice what is different from what they have previously experienced. Difference people constantly make distinctions.

DIFFERENCE People***:

1. Thrive on change
2. Believe in change for change's sake
3. Prefer jobs with variety and abhor routine jobs and situations
4. If an employee, will stay in a job from 6 months to a year

5. Tend to be the creative entrepreneurs of the world

6. Seek what is unique and revolutionary

*** There are two types of Difference People:

1. Mismatchers: They are the ones who are constantly pointing out exceptions to things. We also refer to them as counter-examplers and they are adept at indicating why things won't work. Mismatchers serve the role of trouble-shooters in our society.

2. Polarity Responders: They are people who always do the opposite of what you tell them to do. They have managed to maintain this trait beyond childhood. Reverse psychology works well in dealing with this type of person (much like parents with their children who are going through this phase).

QUALIFIED DIFFERENCE

Qualified Difference People will first notice differences and then similarities in a given situation or experience.

QUALIFIED DIFFERENCE People:

1. Like change in their lives with occasional elements of similarity

2. Need some diversity to spark their continued interest in a job or situation

3. Are the tweakers of the world: creatively making small, quantitative changes

4. Tend to stay in their jobs from 12 months to 2 years depending on the amount of variety they can experience

5. Need some change yet not revolutionary change like pure *Difference* People

6. Prefer to change tasks fairly frequently in their jobs

POPULATION DISTRIBUTION

Sameness: 5 to 10%

Qualified Sameness: 55%

Difference: 5 to 10%

Qualified Difference: 25%

TARGET INDICATOR QUESTIONS

What is the relationship between what you are doing now and what you were doing a month ago?

What is the relationship between what you want from your current job and what you wanted from your previous job?

GENERAL PATTERN: What is the relationship between this X and the previous X?

IDENTIFICATION

Sameness People

1. Always tell you how things are the same
2. Point out similarities between or among the elements
3. Discuss how things haven't changed
4. Talk about commonality of experience

Qualified Sameness People

1. First tell you how things are similar and then mention the differences between or among the elements or situations
2. Point out how things have gradually changed over time
3. Say that "things have improved or are better" or "it is basically the same" or "it is the same except that…"

4. Tend to use comparatives such as *more, less, better than*

Difference People

1. Always indicate the differences between or among the elements or situations
2. Tend to make creative distinctions
3. Will say that the elements being compared are totally different
4. Use words such as unique, different, distinctive, new and revolutionary

Qualified Difference People

1. First indicate the differences between or among the elements or situations and will then point out the similarities
2. Emphasize the difference while noting the similarities in passing
3. Make distinctions to a lesser degree than pure *Difference* people
4. Say, for example, "Things are basically different except for…"

EXAMPLES

Sameness:

1. Things are the same.
2. Everything looks the same.
3. The amount of work is the same now as it was before.
4. I am doing the same thing in my job that I was doing several months ago (or two years ago or whatever).
5. I am still working at the same employer with the same schedule every day.

Qualified Sameness:

1. The job is basically the same except that I am now working with a new client.

2. I am involved in similar projects as I was before, but I have now switched to a different office in the same city, so there are new colleagues.

3. I am doing more of _____ and less of _____.

4. My job duties are close to what I was doing last year, although I have more responsibility now with a larger team.

5. I still have the same job, but I can be more creative in project development.

Difference:

1. The job is totally different from what it was when I started.

2. I am involved in doing entirely new tasks.

3. What I am doing now is dramatically different from what I was doing before in every way.

4. I am working on developing a product that is really unique.

5. I love my constantly changing work environment.

Qualified Difference:

1. The job description is different although I am working in the same office and have the same boss as before.

2. My co-workers have changed with the new owner but I have managed to keep the same job.

3. What I am doing now is better than before in that I have more leeway in how I approach the tasks yet I work the same hours.

4. I visit new clients every week but present the same product line.

5. My job is more varied now than before, although I work with basically the same people.

UTILIZATION GUIDE

SALES

THE CHANGE PEOPLE PATTERN™

Sameness:

1. Stress how your product or service is the same as what they have experienced before (or previously used).
2. Point out the similarities between the products or services.
3. Emphasize how they will be comfortable having a familiar experience.
4. Avoid discussing the differences between the products or services.
5. Don't count on their willingness to change.

Qualified Sameness

1. Frame your product or service as fundamentally the same as what they have experienced or are used to having, although it has been refined or upgraded in some way.
2. Be aware that these people want their products and services to be the same as before, although with improvement in some area.
3. They want to remain in a familiar product/service world that provides them with a measurable comfort zone yet incorporates some change.
4. Talk about the similarities first and then emphasize gradual, evolutionary change with the product or service you are offering.
5. Remember that these people respond well to things that are presented as "improved, better, or slightly more advanced" and tend to resist things that are totally new and different.

Difference:

1. Emphasize how the product or service is completely different from their previous one.
2. Avoid mentioning areas of commonality.
3. Make many distinctions.
4. Frame the product or service as unique and revolutionary (in its features, form, appearance or other pertinent and contextually relevant aspect).
5. Avoid discussing the features or aspects that have not changed.

Qualified Difference:

1. Point out differences first in relation to what is on the market or to what they already have, and then discuss the similarities with what they already have or with what is out there.
2. Frame your product or service as fundamentally different from their prior experience with it except that it has retained some feature or aspect from the previous one.
3. Stress that it is a product or service that has been changed, refined or upgraded in a significant way from other ones in the marketplace.
4. Emphasize new features that improve upon the existing product our service, yet still work well with the prior ones.
5. Avoid talking about the product as totally revolutionary.

MANAGEMENT

Sameness:

1. Make sure that you emphasize continuity and job stability.
2. Have these people do the same tasks the same way all the time.
3. Once they learn how to do a job or execute a task, they will often prefer to do it forever.
4. Don't expect Sameness employees to change the way they do something or even to change their tasks on their own.
5. They have a "don't fix what isn't broken" attitude.

Qualified Sameness:

1. Stress the notion of gradual, slow improvement over time.
2. Have these people engage in the same tasks with some changes now and then.
3. Emphasize stability with some built-in change.
4. Once they learn how to execute a task or do a specific job, they will want to continue doing it for many years as long as some variety is inherent in the job.
5. Make sure that any change is evolutionary.

Difference:

1. Avoid routine tasks and habitual schedules.
2. Emphasize what is unique and different about the job.
3. Encourage their personal creativity.
4. Promote new approaches and new ways of handling situations and tasks to avoid boredom.
5. Don't expect them to do the same job over and over.

Qualified Difference:

1. Emphasize refinements and improvements on the job and downplay commonalities.
2. Change tasks frequently.
3. Managers need to play down similarities.
4. Vary the overall projects and inject an element of familiarity as well.
5. Promote gradual change in the job without radical new approaches.

LANGUAGE TO INFLUENCE

Sameness: in common, maintain, equal, keep the same, same, same as, like, identical, equivalent, in a similar way, retain, familiar, maintain, similar to, hold on to, corresponding, comparable, alike, continue, one and the same, sustain, related to; preserve.

Qualified Sameness: the same except for, the same except that, more, better, less, the same but, the same although, evolved, refined, gradual, evolutionary, enhance, enhancement, bit by bit, improve, improvement; advance, step up; progress.

Difference: unique, inimitable, different, new, revolutionary, radical, one of a kind, distinctive, innovative, avant-garde, unmatched, unlike, variety, innovative, inventive, re-structure, creative, unusual, pioneering, novel, groundbreaking, ingenious, original.

Qualified Difference: changed, modified, new, different, refined, customized, tailored, is different except for; is different but, is different except that;

Chapter III

THE ORGANIZATION PEOPLE PATTERN™

How People experience and organize time and space

Types:

A. Structurists

B. Free Spirits

The **Organization People Pattern**™ has to do with how individuals deal with organization and structure in their lives, in particular with the way in which they structure their time and space, both in a business and personal context. This is significant because the way in which a person organizes his or her time and space directly influences the decision making process. It happens to determine how a person adapts to life in general. This pattern also has interesting repercussions in the traditional 9 to 5 workplace environment, as we shall see.

The two specific Patterns that reflect the ways that people structure their time and space are called *structurist* and *free spirit*.

DESCRIPTION

STRUCTURISTS

Structurists prefer to live their lives according to a set plan. They like to organize and structure their lives from one day to the next with schedules and timetables.

Structurists make life adapt to them. In fact, it is the Structurists who set the rules for the business world; and they do not like it when people try to break the rules.

FREE SPIRITS

Free Spirits, on the other hand, prefer to live their lives spontaneously, as the wind blows, so to speak. They like to have the freedom to do what they want at a given moment. Free Spirits adapt to life. They don't like what they perceive to be rigidity in the traditional business world.

STRUCTURISTS:

1. Prefer to organize their lives according to schedules
2. Make decisions easily and generally stick to them
3. Desire closure
4. Like to be on time and are aware of time
5. Like their space to be orderly and neat
6. Are often viewed as judgmental and stiff by Free Spirits

FREE SPIRITS:

1. Do not like to follow schedules
2. Have difficulty making decisions and often change their minds
3. Avoid closure
4. Prefer to be carefree and are often late, with little awareness of time
5. Are inclined to work/live in rather untidy and messy space
6. Are often viewed as unreliable and flighty by Structurists

POPULATION DISTRIBUTION

Structurists: 50%

Free Spirits 50%

TARGET INDICATOR QUESTIONS

Do you like to live your life according to a plan or to live your life spontaneously?

Are you usually early or on time for appointments and meetings?

Do you get frustrated or angry when others are late?

Do you often change your mind once you've made a decision?

Does it matter if your office or home is neat or messy?

IDENTIFICATION

Structurists

1. Talk about living an organized life, according to a plan
2. Make lists and create schedules
3. Show up early or on time for meetings and appointments
4. Expect others to be on time
5. Prefer to have rules and regulations
6. Don't change their minds unless data warrants it
7. Prefer tidy and neat

Free Spirits

1. Say that they like to live life spontaneously
2. Abhor lists and agendas
3. Are often late
4. Don't mind if others don't abide by appointment times
5. Detest the structure of rules and regulations
6. Easily change their minds at the spur of the moment
7. Tend to be disorganized and live/work in cluttered space

EXAMPLES

Structurists:

1. I prefer to have a plan for whatever I do.

2. I like to schedule things in advance.

3. I make decisions easily and only change my mind when a situation warrants it.

4. I get quite annoyed when people are late.

5. I don't like it when I am late (usually beyond my control).

6. Rules are necessary for order.

7. I really dislike a messy office.

Free Spirits:

1. I really dislike schedules.

2. I definitely don't use or need to use a time management program.

3. Time frames are a waste…I'll get there when I get there.

4. It certainly doesn't bother me if others are late.

5. I hate having to decide on anything final since things can change.

6. I hate the rigidity of rules.

7. I don't mind working in clutter…not a big deal.

UTILIZATION GUIDE

SALES

Structurists:

1. Make your sales presentation in an organized and systematic manner.

2. Begin and end the meeting on time.

3. Be decisive and get closure.

4. Expect a yes or no answer.

5. If you get a no, don't expect a change in decision until you've presented new information or data.

6. Be neat in appearance and in your office space (if you are meeting in your office).

Free Spirits:

1. Avoid insisting on a set schedule or plan for the sales presentation.

2. Show flexibility of behavior.

3. Don't insist on punctuality.

4. Point out the options available.

5. Don't expect a decision.

6. Be sure to future pace to avoid buyer's remorse.

MANAGEMENT

Structurists:

1. Give instructions in a logical and orderly manner.

2. Present a specific schedule and expect punctuality.

3. Explain rules and regulations and expect compliance.

4. To change their minds, make sure to present relevant new data.

5. Avoid last minute changes to a pre-arranged schedule.

6. Present deadlines.

Free Spirits:

1. Emphasize alternatives and present the options from the start.

2. Avoid a rigid schedule and don't expect punctuality.

3. Expect indecisiveness and what may be perceived as irresponsibility.

4. Don't expect them to stick to schedules.

5. Realize that they will change their minds often.

6. Avoid specific deadlines.

LANGUAGE TO INFLUENCE

Structurists

Schedule, deadline, systematize, plan, organize, punctual, on the dot, prompt, definite, order, decisive, time management, fixed, decide, control, organized, closure, resolved, decided, tidiness, arrange, resolute, structured, on time, rules and regulations to follow, agenda, punctuality.

Free Spirits

Spontaneous, undefined, open-ended, relaxed, pending, adaptable, wait and see, flexible, unstructured, accommodate, unrestricted, play the waiting game, as the spirit moves you, go with the flow, impulsive, what deadline?

Chapter IV

THE ACTIVITY PEOPLE PATTERN™

How people engage in activity

Types:

A. Procedures

B. Options

The **Activity People Pattern**™ reveals how a person engages in activity. There are some people who simply can't function in life if they are not specifically told or shown how to do something. They are people who engage in sequential or linear activity and are called *procedural* people. On the other side of the coin, there are individuals who get upset when you begin telling them or showing them how to do something. These people engage in simultaneous activity and are called *options* people.

Options and Procedures represent two totally different ways in which people process information to engage in any given activity or situation. The typical day at the office involves a myriad of activities and circumstances. And your particular **Activity People Pattern**™ will shine through in all that you do in your job on a daily basis, reflecting a multitude of applications and consequences in the workplace. For example, we will show you how Options people and Procedural people buy differently and must be approached and sold to in a different way from a sales perspective.

DESCRIPTION

OPTIONS

These people view activity and learning a task as a simultaneous grouping of different steps that are not in any predetermined or set order. Options people like to have a multitude of alternatives at their disposal to deal with a given activity or situation.

PROCEDURES

These people view activity and learning a task as a sequential series of steps. They can only engage in an activity or deal with a situation by following a clear set of instructions, and furthermore, by following them in a particular order.

OPTIONS People:

1. Process information in a simultaneous manner
2. Prefer to have options available to them to handle any given task or situation
3. Are the ones who create the procedures
4. Have a hard time following procedures
5. Try to improve upon or else deviate from a given procedure even if it works
6. Tend to be less rigid than procedural people in dealing with situations

PROCEDURAL People:

1. Process information in a linear manner
2. Can only engage in an activity or situation by following a procedure
3. Are not able to generate procedures
4. Get stuck and are unable to proceed when a procedure breaks down or doesn't work
5. Often have a compulsive need to complete a given procedure
6. Have only one "right way" of doing something

POPULATION DISTRIBUTION

Options: 50%

Procedures: 50%

TARGET INDICATOR QUESTIONS

Why did you choose your current job?

Why did you choose your current car?

Why did you choose your current laptop?

GENERAL PATTERN: Why did you choose X?

IDENTIFICATION

Options People

1. Will give you reasons as to why they did what they did
2. Will talk about choosing their options and also expanding their options
3. Will answer the "why" question as a "why" question

Procedural People

1. Will tell you a story as to how they came to do what they did
2. Will give the impression that are either unable to make choices or else that they didn't have a choice in the matter
3. Will answer the "why" question as a "how to" question

EXAMPLES

Options People:

1. My job is lots of fun, is challenging and provides many opportunities to travel.
2. My job is exciting and pays extremely well.
3. My car has a good lease program and a dealer with excellent service.
4. My laptop is fast, light and easy to pack into in-flight bags.

Procedural People:

1. I had a friend who told me about a new software company that moved to my area. Since I was looking for a job closer to my home, I called them, had an interview and talked to some of the employees. They gave me a tour of the headquarters. I really liked them and the location. Well, I got the job and accepted it.
2. I was in the market for a new car so I thought I'd check out some of the dealers near the mall. I stopped at the first dealership along the way and got to test drive a few new cars. I never got to the other dealerships since I decided to buy one there that I really liked. I then got the paperwork approved and the car is mine.
3. I was sitting next to a guy during my commuter train ride the other day and I noticed his laptop. I asked him some questions about it and he let me fiddle with it for a few minutes. That evening I went to the computer store to check it out for myself. The salesperson showed me how to use this particular model and I was hooked.

UTILIZATION GUIDE

SALES

Options:

1. Emphasize how your product will expand their options and provide interesting alternatives.

2. Discuss the various possibilities available.

3. Be sure to give reasons why the prospective customer is to buy your product.

4. Tell them that you will bend the rules for them.

5. Avoid following a fixed agenda or procedure.

6. Make sure that there are not a lot of forms to fill out.

Procedures:

1. Make of point of presenting the procedures involved in using the product and also in buying the product.

2. Avoid giving any options.

3. Present each sequential step of the process (ex. Let's explain the exact procedure for….)

4. Explain that the procedure for them to buy it has already begun and that they are in fact, part way through it.

5. They are compelled to complete the procedure and will buy the product because it is one of the steps of the entire procedure.

6. Make sure that signing the contract or using the credit card is a middle step in the procedure with the final step being their having used the product and their calling you to thank you.

MANAGEMENT

Options:

1. Emphasize the possibilities and alternative ways to proceed.

2. Expect that Options people will not follow procedures.

3. Remember that they will violate procedures whenever they can.

4. Tell them that you are flexible and are not stuck on rules.

5. Know that they will always want to come up with better ways to do things.

6. Avoid mentioning procedures since that will create tension.

Procedures:

1. Emphasize the procedures needed to work on a project or deal with a situation.

2. Be specific and present each step of the procedure.

3. Make sure that the Procedural person thoroughly understands the procedure backwards and forwards.

4. Point out that this is the "right way" to do it and how it is to be done.

5. Definitely be prepared to help them if the procedure breaks down.

6. Avoid changing established procedures since that will create stress.

LANGUAGE TO INFLUENCE

Options

Choices, alternatives, options, reasons, why to, possibilities, another way, another, substitute, other ways, opportunities, replacement, alternate approach, potential, freedom of choice.

Procedures

Right way, procedure, proven way, how to, correct way, exact way, accurate instructions, follow directions, instructions, only way.

Chapter V

THE MOTIVE PEOPLE PATTERN™

The Specific Carrots and Sticks of Motivation

Types:

A. Power

B. Affiliation

C. Achievement

We have already presented the **Motivation People Pattern™** which is the basis of why anyone does anything in life. As we have explained earlier, a person is either Move Toward in orientation and is, thus, motivated by carrots or else a person is Move Away From in orientation and is motivated by sticks.

Knowing a person's Motivation People Pattern™ is only part of the picture, however. We must also be able to identify what particular carrots and sticks to use in motivating oneself and others. This is because to motivate effectively, you need to know precisely what carrots and sticks to use and which ones correspond to the different contexts in a person's life.

The carrots and sticks are what we call **motives**. Different circumstances and contexts may require a variety of carrots and sticks. This is critically important because choosing the wrong stick or carrot in a situation or interaction may end up triggering the opposite behavior than the one you would like to encourage.

A person's motives will be one of the following three things: 1) **power** 2) **affiliation** or 3) **achievement**. Everyone has one of these motives which is the primary driving force in their lives, and another one that is secondary. An individual is either going to *move toward* or *move away from* in one of these three areas (Later we will see that business comes out of an achievement orientation.).

DESCRIPTION

POWER

The major focus of Power people is to accrue and to maintain power. Control is the important issue in their lives, whether it be their control over other people, situations, things or events. As such, dominance and submission are key factors for them. They perceive all human interactions as power struggles and contests of will, either physical or mental or both.

AFFILIATION

The main concern of Affiliation people is relationships. They perceive all human interactions in terms of whether they create or destroy positive relationships. Affiliation people are motivated to create or improve relationships and oppose those who threaten good relationships. Issues of inclusion and exclusion are important to them.

ACHIEVEMENT

The principal focus of Achievement people is accomplishment. Success is the major factor in their lives and they oppose anything and anyone that gets in the way of their success. They have a strong desire to achieve their goals and to succeed in whatever they do, no matter what the context, in their personal or professional lives.

POWER People:

1. Are motivated to exert power over others and to be in control
2. Evaluate people as to whether they support or oppose them
3. Oppose any threat to their control or influence
4. Enjoy competition and competitive sports
5. Can be highly manipulative to get what they want

AFFILIATION People:

1. Have a strong need for friendly and close interpersonal relationships
2. Want relationships that are based on mutual understanding
3. Evaluate people as to whether they are nice to them or not
4. Prefer cooperation to competition
5. Want to promote harmony and friendship

ACHIEVEMENT People:

1. Are driven to constantly do things better and to excel at what they do
2. Evaluate others on the basis of their accomplishments
3. Don't particularly like lazy people or those with no drive
4. Are quality and performance oriented
5. Have the ability to prioritize tasks to achieve their goals

POPULATION DISTRIBUTION

Power: 33.3%

Affiliation: 33.3%

Achievement: 33.3%

TARGET INDICATOR QUESTIONS

With whom do you get along best and least and why?

Why did you do what you did today?

Tell me about your favorite activity?

INDENTIFICATION

Power People

1. Will tell you how they take control of situations and of people
2. Will discuss conflict issues and power struggles within their organization, team, family, etc.
3. Will express their pride at winning arguments
4. Will be highly competitive
5. Will focus on themselves

Affiliation People

1. Will talk about their personal relationships
2. Will love to talk about the people they care about
3. Will not be confrontational or competitive
4. Will concentrate on others rather than on themselves
5. Will focus on means rather than on ends

Achievement People

1. Will talk about their accomplishments on a given day, week, etc.
2. Will discuss their goals
3. Will present their priorities and discuss how they set them
4. Will be task oriented
5. Will focus on ends rather than on means

EXAMPLES

Power People:

1. I don't enjoy spending time with spineless people, although they are certainly easy to manipulate.
2. Today I met with the staff and basically imposed my viewpoint and action plan, since I don't really care what they think about it.
3. I confronted my boss because I didn't like the way that he was handling certain issues on the job.
4. I really enjoy playing competitive sports because I love beating everyone.

Affiliation People:

1. My favorite pastime is just being with close friends and family since they are the center of my world.
2. I love doing a good job because it pleases my spouse (coach, boss, best friend, etc.) so much.
3. What matters most in my work is that my employer appreciates what I do for her.
4. I really don't like being around people who aren't nice.

Achievement People:

1. What exactly did you accomplish today? I got a lot done myself.
2. Today I met with my Board of Directors, had a staff meeting, had lunch with two new clients and worked on our annual budget.
3. I don't have patience with employees who don't meet deadlines and who don't care about our company's goals so I let them go.
4. I am in the midst of organizing a conference for entrepreneurs that is going to make them even more successful and productive.

UTILIZATION GUIDE

SALES

Power People:

1. Always look for the best deal and one where they are not exploited
2. Don't like to be sold on anything
3. Want to be in charge of the sales interaction
4. Will always want to negotiate the price and maintain the upper hand
5. Don't care about win/win interactions

Affiliation People:

1. Tend to buy from individuals and firms that they know and trust
2. Want the salesperson to be genuinely interested in them
3. Often try to make friends with the salesperson
4. See the relationship as more important than the actual sale
5. Will express their feelings during the sales presentation

Achievement People:

1. Are focused on the service and on efficiency
2. Expect the salesperson to be competent and knowledgeable
3. Want direct and to the point communication that doesn't waste time
4. Expect quality products and service
5. Want a win-win sales interaction

MANAGEMENT

Power People:

1. Like to give orders and do things their way
2. Expect obedience from their employees and co-workers

3. Engage in conflict for the sake of conflict

4. Only take orders from those who yield more power

5. Easily threaten, punish and fire people when they feel like it

Affiliation People:

1. Expect others to like them and to appreciate them

2. Are great charmers

3. Are not comfortable with conflict or negative situations

4. Will go out of their way to be friendly with people

5. Believe that teamwork and collaboration are key elements to success

Achievement People:

1. Promote goals, objectives and long and short term plans

2. Thrive on accomplishing tasks and goals and expect others to do the same

3. Focus on productivity rather than on relationships and personal interaction

4. Don't like teams unless they can achieve goals and high performance levels

5. Focus on creating quality products and services

LANGUAGE TO INFLUENCE

Power People

Manipulate, control, crush, dictate, vanquish, overpower, dominate, win, defeat, take over, coerce, influence, rule over, demand, compel, punish, take charge of, command, overthrow, conquer, order, force, authority, beat, threaten, intimidate, pressure, bully, rout.

Affiliation People

Harmony, friendship, care, concern, fame, family, friends, relationships, significant other, cooperation, associates, teams, teamwork, solidarity, group effort, relations, union, humanistic, connections, coalition, agreement, associations, accord, collaboration, alliance, maintenance.

Achievement People

Success, accomplishment, expert, expertise, realize, accomplish, attain, mission, objective, purpose, task, assignment, skilled, aim, ambition, knowledgeable, proficient, achieve, get, obtain, performance, productivity, performance enhancement, quality, TQM, produce, efficiency, competent, competency, effectiveness, accomplished, experienced, function, capable, undertaking, ability.

Chapter VI

THE EVALUATION PEOPLE PATTERN™

How people make judgments about themselves and their world

Types

A. External Referential Filter

B. Internal Referential Filter

The **Evaluation People Pattern™** reveals the different ways in which an individual evaluates a situation, a person, an experience, a thing or anything else in life for that matter. If you think about it, one of the most fundamental of all human activities is that of making judgments.

In the context of our discussion here, when we refer to judgments, we are referring not to a moral judgment, but rather to what criteria people use to base their decisions. If we ask people how they know that what they are doing or saying or thinking is right, they will respond in one of two ways: they will either use what we refer to as **internal** criteria or **external** criteria.

We call the criteria that a person uses to make judgments his or her referential filters. Individuals who base their decisions on *internal* criteria have what we call an **Internal Evaluation People Pattern™**. They base their actions and decisions on what they know inside to be right or appropriate. Those who base their decisions on external criteria have an **External Evaluation People Pattern™**. They base their actions and decisions on what other people think or do.

There are also some people who have primary internal referential filters and may use external data to decide or modify a decision. In this case, we say that they have an **Internal Evaluation People Pattern™** with an **external check** that is contextual in nature. On the other hand, there are also those who make decisions based on what others say or do and then combine it with an internal verification. They have an **External Evaluation People Pattern™** with an **internal check** that is contextual in nature.

DESCRIPTION

INTERNAL People

Internal people evaluate things on the basis of what they, themselves think is right or appropriate. They make their own decisions without the influence of other opinions.

EXTERNAL People

External people make evaluations based on what other people think or say is right or appropriate. They are incapable of making decisions without the influence of other people's opinions.

Internal People:

1. Provide their own motivation
2. Make their own decision independently of others
3. Always decide what they want to do and how they are going to do it without the influence of others
4. May get information from other sources yet always decide for themselves
5. Have a hard time accepting other people's feedback and guidance

External People:

1. Need other people to provide motivation and direction
2. Are incapable of deciding for themselves
3. Decide on a plan of action and what they are going to do based on the opinion of other people
4. Constantly need feedback from others as to how they are doing

5. Have a hard time starting a task or project or even completing a task without ongoing feedback and guidance from other people

POPULATION DISTRIBUTION

Internal: 50%

External: 50%

TARGET INDICATOR QUESTIONS

How do you know when you've done a good job?

How do you know that you've chosen the right bank?

How do you know that you are right?

GENERAL PATTERN: How do you know that you have done a good job choosing X or doing X?

IDENTIFICATION

Internal People

1. Will tell you that they just know inside that they've done a good job or have chosen the right bank, computer, etc

2. Will say that they don't need others to tell them whether they've done a good job or have made the right choice about something or someone

3. Will tell you that they decide that they are right

4. Will get annoyed if someone tries to make a decision for them

5. May take in information about something and will ultimately make the decision themselves without outside influence

External People

1. Will tell you that they know because other people have told them
2. Will say that other people have made the decisions for them and that they accept their decisions
3. Will say that their employer always tell them that they are doing a good job
4. Will say that they are uncomfortable making decisions without help from others
5. Will tell you that they need external feedback and opinions to decide anything

EXAMPLES

Internal People:

1. I am my own judge of things.
2. I don't look to others for approval.
3. I just know that I am right.
4. I know that I am doing a good job because it is an inner knowing.
5. I couldn't care less about what other people think.

External People:

1. I know that I am doing a good job because my boss tells me.
2. I have friends who bought that computer so I did also.
3. What other people think about what I do really matters to me.
4. I like being reminded that what I am doing is right.
5. I don't buy a product unless it is recommended to me by a friend or someone who has bought it and said it is a good product.

UTILIZATION GUIDE

SALES

Internal People:

1. Emphasize that you can't sell them and that they have to decide for themselves whether to buy the product or service.
2. Suggest that they do their internal check to make the decision.
3. Tell them that you know that they will know inside what to do about the sale.
4. Know that they want to decide for themselves and don't need to hear your opinion.
5. Refrain from giving testimonials or telling them who else bought the product because they don't care.

External People:

1. Provide lots of referral material.
2. Give as many testimonials as possible.
3. Emphasize what other people think about your product or service.
4. Quote data and statistics.
5. Have group presentations whenever possible because they will buy when they see others buying the product.

MANAGEMENT

Internal People:

1. You don't need to give feedback or even praise.
2. Avoid managing them since they won't like it.
3. Refrain from giving your opinion about a decision to be made.
4. Stress how your goals are aligned with theirs.
5. Don't tell them what to do since they'll decide for themselves.

External People:

1. You have to manage them closely.
2. You need to tell them what to do and then give them feedback about how they are doing at the job or task.

3. Provide constant supervision and feedback with either praise or criticism as is contextually appropriate.

4. Help them to set their performance goals.

5. Give them specific examples of correct performance.

LANGUAGE TO INFLUENCE

Internal People:

Only you can decide. What have you decided? I agree with you. You will ultimately make the right decision. Why don't you decide? It is up to you. I know that you don't need my opinion. I know that you will know what to do. I have confidence that you know what to do about this. You will decide based on what you think. I know that you don't care about what other people are saying about this.

External People:

Other people think that… Others are saying that… This is the way it is. Here is the feedback that I can give you. You are really doing a great job (or whatever is appropriate) to the situation. I will let you know how it is going. Here is my opinion. The facts show that… This is what everyone is saying… I know that what your boss (family, friends, etc.) thinks about this is important to you.

Chapter VII

THE PRIMARY INTEREST

PEOPLE PATTERN™

A gauge for a person's main focus in life

Types:

A. People

B. Place

C. Things

D. Activity

E. Information

There are two **People Patterns™** which focus on information in the context of communication. In this chapter, we discuss the **Primary Interest People Pattern™**, which deals with the **content** of the information we provide in a given communication exchange. (As we shall see in the following chapter of this book, the other pattern, is actually called the **Information People Pattern™** because it deals with 1) the way in which we internally represent the information in our minds and 2) the way in which we structure information in our communication.)

Here our discussion of the **Primary Interest People Pattern™** centers on the main content of a person's communication. It deals with the area of life which is of greatest interest to us. This Pattern explains why we find some people interesting and others boring. All of us have been in situations in which we seem to hit it off with certain people and not with others. The reason for this match or mismatch is based on the **Primary Interest People Pattern™**.

Furthermore, there are certain things in life which attract our attention and upon which we focus. What we do, where we spend our time, with whom we pass our time, what books we read, how we spend our money, all of these factors are based on the **Primary Interest People Pattern™**.

Although there are many different interests in life, these interests fall in five main categories. These areas correspond to the classes of nouns. By definition, a noun is a word that is a person, place, thing, activity or quality or concept. Thus, the **Primary Interest People Pattern™** is comprised of the following elements:

1. People

2. Place

3. Thing

4. Activity

5. Information (which is a about a concept or condition)

People will usually have a Primary Interest People Pattern™, and then a second interest, and at times, a third interest.

DESCRIPTION

PEOPLE People

Individuals whose **Primary Interest Pattern™** is People are predominately interested in people. Their basic question is "Who?" They will also be curious to know "about whom." The people in their world may be family members, friends, business associates, celebrities or total strangers.

PLACE People

Place people are primarily interested in location or place. Their primary question is "Where?" They will also focus on "about where?" Place may take the form of their home or office, some place where they would like to be. Places are ordered in space.

THE PRIMARY INTEREST PEOPLE PATTERN™

THING People

Thing people are interested in objects or things. Their primary question is "What?" They also desire to know "about what?" The objects and things which interest them may be functional, monetarily valuable, practical, decorative or of personal meaning and emotion-laden.

ACTIVITY People

Activity people are focused on activities, on doing, and on events and happenings. Their primary question will be "How" and also "When?" In addition, they will want to know "about how?" Their activities and events may occur in the context of home, work, hobbies and recreation.

INFORMATION People

Information people are interested in what else but information, and all aspects of information for that matter. They will want to know "What?"; "Where?"; "Why?"; "When?"; "How"; and "Who?" Information people will also want to know the "about" aspect of these elements. Their primary focus is on the concepts, qualities and conditions associated with these elements.

People People:

1. Enjoy doing things that relate to other people
2. Express their interest in people by either talking to them or by wanting to be with them
3. Always mention the names of people in their conversations whether relevant or not
4. Have a need for frequent interaction with other people
5. Are secondarily interested in where people are doing things (place), in the objects with which people are associated (thing), in what other people are doing (activity) or else in gossip about other people (information)

Place People:

1. Always focus on location and on where they are at a given time
2. Put a priority on place over activity, people, things and information
3. Focus on where they are going, whether it be their home, office or event
4. Place importance on indoor or outdoor locations
5. Are secondarily interested in who is there (people), in what is there (thing), in what is happening there (activity) or in descriptions of places (information)

Thing People:

1. Focus on the material aspects of the world
2. Tend to be the collectors of the world
3. Purchase things not based on need, but on what they want to have
4. Enjoy buying, possessing, owning, collecting and exchanging things
5. Are secondarily interested in who is associated with the thing (people), in where the thing is located (place), in how the thing is used (activity) or in descriptions of the thing (information)

Activity People:

1. Focus their lives around actions, activities, events and happenings
2. Choose to engage in activities as either active participants or as observers
3. Love to move and to sense their bodies in motion
4. Find it difficult to be still and are always involved in doing something
5. Are secondarily interested in who is engaging in a given activity (people), where it is happening (place), what equipment is being used in the activity (thing) or in descriptions of the activity or event (information)

Information People:

1. Focus on the obtaining, on the learning and on the giving of information
2. Want to know everything possible about something
3. Thrive on quality facts, data and information

THE PRIMARY INTEREST PEOPLE PATTERN™

4. Tend to be selective as to the source of information they acquire as well as with whom they will share any given information

5. Are secondarily interested in information about people (in the form of gossip or news), in information about things (catalogs and descriptions), in information about activities (guides and "how to" manuals), or in information about information (references)

POPULATION DISTRIBUTION

People: 35%

Place: 5%

Thing: 25%

Activity: 30%

Information: 5%

TARGET INDICATOR QUESTIONS

Tell me about a recent experience you had.

Tell me about your day.

Tell me about your favorite restaurant and why you like it.

IDENTIFICATION

People People

1. Will talk about the people with whom they personally interacted or with whom they were dealing in a given experience

2. Will talk about other people who were involved in a given experience even if they themselves were not involved in it

3. Will mention the names of people in describing their day, an event, etc.

4. Will go out of their way to show you photographs of their family, friends and of significant people in their lives and often have many photographs in their office of both people they know and don't know

5. Will describe the people with whom they were at a restaurant and will also focus on their interactions with the waiters and restaurant staff, providing names when they can

Place People

1. Will tell you where they were on a given day or regarding a particular experience

2. Will tell you where other people were in describing an experience or their day, both in relation to them and to the event or experience

3. Will discuss the ambiance of the place in describing their day or a specific experience

4. Will have photographs of places they have been or places they would like to visit in their home or office

5. Will talk about the feel of a particular restaurant, describing where it is located and where they were sitting

Thing People

1. Will tell you about things or objects in describing their day or a specific experience

2. Will tell you about things other people had or were using in that experience

3. Will be focused on describing specific objects or things which caught their attention (and which naturally stand out in their minds)

4. Will tend to have lots of things and objects in their office, and more if they are collectors of a particular thing

5. Will discuss the things in a restaurant, such as the chairs, table, flowers in the room and other things that spark their Primary penchant

THE PRIMARY INTEREST PEOPLE PATTERN™

Activity People

1. Will describe exactly what they were doing on a given day or in relating a particular experience

2. Will focus on what other people were doing on that day or in describing an experience

3. Will tell you when activities occurred or when events happened

4. Will have equipment and items that reflect their activity sort, such as golf clubs or tennis rackets in their office

5. Will describe the restaurant in terms of the movement and activity of the staff (how good the service was) and in terms of what they (the customers) did before, during and after the meal

Information People

1. Will tell you about the concepts, the quality, the conditions which relate to people, place, things, activity and information

2. Will focus on describing pertinent and useful information that provides clarity and understanding to a given experience

3. Will have lots of books in their office

4. Will discuss interesting and enlightening information obtained in conversation or in observation while at a restaurant

5. Are focused on learning something from an experience and gathering useful information rather than on arbitrarily describing the people, place, thing, activity or information

EXAMPLES

People People:

1. Today I had a full schedule meeting with the new team members --- Sophia, Woody, James, and Andrew. They were all aligned with the mission. We were pleasantly surprised to find out that we had mutual acquaintances in Jon and Darlene.

2. One of the more interesting conferences I attended recently, involved interacting closely with the other attendees and networking with some of the more successful small business entrepreneurs in the country...the highlight of which was my having lunch with Rob M___, the operations director for PRO___ which is now the most successful and wide-reaching information marketing organization in the country.

3. Last evening, we had dinner with the two top salespeople in our organization, Ryan and Lynne, and their respective spouses, Suzanne and Adam. Joe, the restaurant's *maitre d'* treated us exceptionally well.

Place People:

1. Last week, we had our annual meeting at the Ritz Carlton because the Conference Room ambiance is quiet and conducive to having productive discussions over a great meal.

2. I walked into the manager's office and saw beautiful photographs of the amazing places she had visited on her many trips around the globe.

3. We ended up going to the best French restaurant in town while visiting the DC area and actually ended up sitting at what is known to be the most desired table in the place; and we somehow managed that without a reservation.

Thing People:

1. For the satellite interview, the CEO wore a black, pin-striped suit with ivory pearls and black patent pumps, a white camellia corsage and a gold chain belt. Her assistant wore a complimentary black and gray tie and a dark gray suit. Both were

carrying fine leather, engraved attachés. They gave out personally engraved golf clubs to the entire staff of the station.

2. The meeting room was full of bronze sculptures from the different artists the boss had met during various business trips to the five continents. Also, on her desk were personally signed letters in glass casing from several world dignitaries with whom she had conducted high level discussions about the economy for the administration.

3. The restaurant last evening had the most elegant décor, with Russian Regency chairs with matching carpeting, beautifully etched, glass table tops, matching molding and the most distinctive collection of modern landscapes that I had ever seen in an eating establishment.

Activity People:

1. We casually walked to the restaurant from the office which is centrally located just minutes from the train station from which most of us commute.

2. We had to wait quite a long time to get into the event. The people organizing it were not very efficient and we lost two hours of time we could have spent still working on the project which we have to finish by next Monday.

3. During our meal we spoke about our hobbies and about how we like to spend our leisurely moments. We ate rather quickly so that we could get back in time to watch the much anticipated tennis match, which is being broadcast both on the Internet and on TV.

Information People:

1. At the conference, we met an interesting couple who have created specific models to teach people how to learn and how to think critically in order to engender fruitful problem-solving and thinking outside of the box.

2. We ended up having quite an informative discussion with the sales team in that we analyzed each person to determine how they became so successful at what they do.

3. The meal turned out to be both instructive and insightful in that our guest provided lots of research-based and relevant information about the toxicity of our food supply

and how to combat it, as well as a wealth of knowledge and data regarding the use of supplements and their realistic contribution to our overall health and well-being.

UITILZATION GUIDE

SALES

People People:

1. Will be focused on the relationships created in the sales interaction
2. Tend to buy from people they know or to buy based on introductions from other people they know and trust
3. Prefer to buy from people they like and tend not to buy from people or companies that they dislike
4. Like to deal with salespeople who go out of their way to connect with them and to establish a relationship
5. Want to hear about celebrity endorsements and about endorsements from people they know in considering a purchase

Place People:

1. Place a priority on the location of the sales presentation
2. Consider the ambiance of the sales meeting to be a vital component of the sale
3. Will frequent stores (and their respective locations) that appeal to them
4. Will go out of their way to avoid locations and stores that they don't like
5. Want to feel comfortable in the physical place in which a sales presentation is made

Thing People:

1. Place an emphasis on what they are buying
2. Either really like or dislike things
3. Are the collectors of the world and buy based on what objects they accumulate in their lives

4. Expect enthusiasm about the things being sold

5. Buy based on the quality of a thing that appeals to them most, whether it be practicality, image and prestige, re-sale value, performance, etc.

Activity People:

1. Tend to buy things that provide functionality in the context of their preferred activity

2. Buy things that support their activities in life

3. Will love buying and shopping if it provides enjoyment

4. Will loathe shopping and buying if it is an activity that interferes with their activity-based schedule

5. Expect salespeople to respect their time and personal schedules

Information People:

1. Want authoritative information about what they buying

2. Expect to have intelligent salespeople with excellent product knowledge

3. Have no patience with ignorant salespeople

4. Tend to ask many questions about what they are buying

5. Dislike salespeople who "fake it" when they obviously don't know anything or very little about a product that they are selling

MANAGEMENT

People People:

1. Work best when managers take time to build relationships with them

2. Will tend to do things for the manager they like

3. Will go out of their way to help or to do things for managers who take an interest in them

4. Tend to spend time with other people in the workplace and are concerned with office morale

5. Like to talk and engage in people-based conversations (gossip)

Place People:

1. Will place importance on where they work
2. Will focus on the physical surroundings and ambiance of the work environment
3. Will only want to commute to locations that are pleasing and/or convenient to them
4. Will change their workspace to make it most comfortable for them
5. Have a productivity factor that is linked to the location of their work as well as their personal work space

Thing People

1. Want to make money to buy things
2. Believe that he or she who amasses the most and best toys in life wins
3. Tend to want the best and latest and most advanced pieces of equipment such as technology
4. Pay attention to maintenance and quality control
5. May lose touch with the real purpose of things in the workplace

Activity People

1. What they do or are doing is of primary importance to them
2. Easily get bored when standing or sitting idly and intensely dislike inactivity
3. Prefer to be "doing" rather than to be thinking
4. Expect managers to give them tasks to complete
5. Prefer jobs that involve action, movement and activity

Information People

1. Expect managers to tell them everything they know regarding their job or any issue that involves their work
2. Will always want lots of information
3. Like to think and reflect on things, people, concepts and situations
4. Expect managers to respect their privacy and alone time

5. Want managers to give them problems to solve on their own without interference from others

LANGUAGE TO INFLUENCE

People People

Who, they, them, we, us, people, individuals, link, the good of all, connection, friendship, for all, rapport, someone, companion, affinity, significant other, relationship, affiliation, union, friends, relatives, family, relations, teammates, community, neighborhood.

Place People

Where, there, here, wherever, location, place, scene, at this place, someplace, somewhere, site, local color, vista, backdrop, view, mood, setting, scenery, locale, ambiance, environment, spot, atmosphere, surroundings, feel for the place, panorama, landscape, milieu.

Thing People

What, thing, object, it, apparatus, equipment, item, article, entity, collection, collector, album, collected works, piece, assortment, worth, material, value of, --- things are expensive, practical, functional, beautiful, rare, ancient, useful, outrageous, funny, outstanding, trendy, state of the art, sacred, uplifting, advanced, etc., depending on their personal taste.

Activity People

How, when, how to (engage in activity), activity, doing, motion, movement, act, episode, achievement, event, happenings, goings on, action, perform, occasion, experience, incidents, do something, operate, work, play, sports, games, schedules, time, cultural events, hobbies, exercise, entertainment.

Information People

Why, facts, information about how to, expertise, expert, data, wisdom, information, capability, statistics, aptitude, ability, knowledge, details, directions, know-how, competency, learn, comprehend, comprehension, specialist, theories, proficiency, skill, command of, authoritative, understanding, models, academics, education, learning, adept.

Chapter VIII

THE INFORMATION PEOPLE PATTERN™

How We Take In Information and How Much

I. How we take in information about the world

Types:

A. Tangible

B. Intangible

II. How much information we take in and communicate back

Types:

A. Global

B. Specific

We have already discussed information from the perspective of the **Primary Interest People Pattern™** which deals with the content of an information exchange or what kind of information is communicated. Now we move on to a different aspect of information which is called the **Information People Pattern™**. It is composed of two elements:

1) our perception and internal representation of the information and
2) the way in which we structure the information.

The first element has to do with how we take in information about the world around us and how we represent the information internally to ourselves. We call it the **Perceptual Source People Pattern™**. As you will see, there are two modes of perception or two ways in which we take in information about the world. The first is through sensory means and is called the ***Tangible Pattern™***. The other is through non-sensory means and is called the ***Intangible Pattern™***.

The second aspect of the **Information People Pattern™** deals with the structure of the information. We refer to it as the **Chunk Size People Pattern™**. In this context, people will either be **global** or **specific**. We will discuss this second aspect of the **Information People Pattern™** in the section following the **Perceptual Source People Pattern™**.

PERCEPTUAL SOURCE:
TANGIBLE AND INTANGIBLE PEOPLE

DESCRIPTION

TANGIBLE People

Tangibles take in information about the world around them by means of their five senses. Consequently, they focus on what they can see, hear, feel, taste and smell. Thus, they want things to be tangible.

INTANGIBLE People

Intangibles take in information about the world around them through non-sensory means. They are thus, highly intuitive and operate out of what may be termed a "sixth sense." They thrive on things and situations that are intangible.

Tangibles:

1. Focus on that which is concrete and factual
2. Concentrate on facts and experiences
3. Need proof of things and events
4. Focus on the present and on the here and now
5. Are the pragmatists of the world

Intangibles:

1. Focus on possibilities and on the meaning of things

2. Approach things holistically and in an abstract manner
3. Don't need proof of things and events
4. Are focused on the future
5. Are the visionaries of the world

POPULATION DISTRIBUTION

Tangibles: 50%

Intangibles 50%

TARGET INDICATOR QUESTIONS

Do you like to have proof of things or are things obvious to you?

Do you make decisions based on what is practical and real or based on conceptual possibilities?

How did your day go?

IDENTIFICATION

Tangibles:

1. Will say that they require proof of things
2. Will say that they don't accept results that are not tangible
3. Will tell you that they prefer things that they can see, hear, touch, feel, taste or smell
4. Will say that they make decisions based on what is practical and viable
5. Will describe their day with details based on their five senses

Intangibles:

1. Will say that they don't require proof of things and events

2. Will say that things are naturally obvious to them

3. Will tell you that they focus on possibilities

4. Will say that their decision making is based on their intuitive take on things and events

5. Will not describe their day in sensory-based details because they consider them to be boring

EXAMPLES

Tangibles:

1. How do you know that?

2. What is the evidence that it works?

3. How is that practical?

4. Are your results based on facts or scientific data?

5. Will provide a minute by minute sensory account of what transpired on a given day: At the meeting today, we heard practical advice and real, everyday examples of how to cope with the current economic situation, and saw lots of data to prove the points covered.

Intangibles:

1. That is quite obvious to me.

2. I don't need proof…I know it works

3. What are the possibilities?

4. I can tell you intuitively that…

5. Will give you a conceptual overview of their day or provide a discourse on life in general: Today's meeting provided an interesting perspective on how to deal with future prospects.

UITILZATION GUIDE

SALES

Tangibles:

1. Have products that they can see, touch and feel.
2. Tell them what your products will realistically do for them.
3. Be factual and concrete in discussing your product or service.
4. Be prepared to provide evidence or proof that the product works and that backs it up.
5. Stress the practical aspects of your product or service.

Intangibles:

1. Stress the possibilities of your product or service.
2. Show how the product or service fits into an overall framework.
3. Avoid boring them with facts and sensory-based information.
4. Tell them about the future possibilities of your product or service.
5. Emphasize the abstract.

MANAGEMENT

Tangibles:

1. Tell them exactly what to do and how to do it.
2. Remind them that your suggestion has been proven to work.
3. Expect them to be good at handling concrete details and administrative tasks.
4. Be concrete and tangible.
5. Don't expect abstract thinking.

Intangibles:

1. Provide them with the big picture and explain how their task or work fits well into that picture.
2. Don't expect them to be adept at managing routine daily activities.
3. Know that they will get bored with details and dry facts.
4. Expect them to be a good source for new ideas.
5. Accept that they are capable of going beyond the obvious.

LANGUAGE TO INFLUENCE

Tangibles:

Realistic, actual, factual, data, reality-based, down to earth, control group, reasonable, tangible, no-nonsense, scientific backing, evidence, proof, existing, fact, practical, verification, pragmatic, based on fact, detailed, present, here and now, concrete, physical, sensory, straightforward, substantiated, empirical.

Intangibles:

Abstract, strategic, intuitive, possibilities, conceptual, universal, speculative, vision, theoretical, ingenuity, futurist, general, insights, insightful, hypothetical, intangible, inspiration, creative thinking, instinctive, wide-ranging, planned, creativity, far-sighted, intuition, supposed, across the board, inspired, visionary, imaginative, imagination, sixth sense.

B. CHUNK SIZE:

GLOBAL AND SPECIFIC PEOPLE

As we mentioned earlier in this section, the second element of the **Information People Pattern™** has to do with the way in which people structure information in a communication exchange. This element of the **Information People Pattern™** reveals the amount of information involved as well as the specificity of the information. It is called the

Chunk Size People Pattern™. The notion of chunking is a powerful one and describes how we break information down into units.

There is a concept in psychology that says that we can pay attention to seven plus or minus chunks of attention at any time. If a person is presented with too much information than he or she can process, the result is overwhelm. The opposite is also true. If a person is presented with too little information or with too few details, the result is either boredom or insufficient information upon which to make a decision. These two examples are the basis of the **Chunk Size People Pattern™**.

The above factors deal with what we refer to as *scope* and *depth*. The scope of the information refers to how many aspects of a given piece of information a person presents. The depth of the information deals with the amount of detail presented relating to any given aspect of the information. When communicating, people will either show a preference for scope or depth. We refer to people who prefer scope of information in communication as *Global*. We refer to those who prefer depth of information in communication as *Specific*.

DESCRIPTION

GLOBAL People

Global people have marked preference for the big picture in the way that they think and communicate. They are much more comfortable with large chunks of information than not. Global people do what we refer to as "chunking up," which means that they go into lesser and lesser detail to consider more scope and less depth.

SPECIFIC People

Specific people prefer details and all that is specific in their thinking and communication. They are most comfortable with small units or chunks of information. In marked contrast to Globals, Specific people "chunk down" when they communicate. This means that they go into greater and greater detail to consider more depth and less scope.

Global People:

1. Prefer the broad overview
2. Will always provide you with the big picture or overall framework
3. See the forest for the trees
4. Conceive of a whole project at once
5. Consider details to be insignificant or irrelevant

Specific People:

1. Like to give small details
2. Are capable of understanding small pieces of data
3. See the trees for the forest
4. Have difficulty making sense of a larger picture
5. Consider global perspectives to be shallow and superficial

POPULATION DISTRIBUTION

Global: 50%

Specific 50%

TARGET INDICATOR QUESTIONS

Tell me what you would like to do today.

Do you prefer to discuss the big picture first or to have the details first?

What would you like to know about this project?

General Pattern: Listen to any sentence that they utter.

IDENTIFICATION

Global People:

1. Will present a general overview of a situation without giving details
2. Will ask for a general plan with few details and no minutia
3. Tend to speak using simple grammatical structures without lots of prepositional phrases
4. Will often describe things in no particular order
5. Will want to skip ahead when provided with too many details

Specific People:

1. Will provide all the details
2. Will use lots of extra modifiers in their descriptions
3. Will return to the initial step when interrupted
4. Will chunk down several levels in their explanations
5. Will describe things in a particular sequence

EXAMPLES

Global People:

1. I would like to find a job near my home and one that is close to a bank that provides high interest and close to some grocery chain and pet food store.
2. All of us went to dinner finally.

Specific People:

1. I want a job that is within 10 miles of my home, preferably west of my present location so that I can avoid the morning and evening rush hour traffic between 7 and 10 am, and that is close to the Clover Leaf Center, which has Krowl Pharmacy,

Exquisite Pet Foods, Super Tech Store, Healthy Cuisine Shop, and Readers Choice Books, and where I have a 24 hour GFA banking center that provides 4% interest on my checking and savings accounts, and which is near my Best Warehouse, which provides the best gas prices in my area.

2. Last night, my husband and I went to dinner at Dee's Steak Supreme on Allen Pike, with Wayne and his wife, Anne, from my last software design job; and we ordered an excellent lobster bisque as well as a Cesar salad, along with incredibly tender, medium rib-eye steaks, creamed spinach, garlic mashed potatoes and then vanilla ice cream with berries for dessert.

UITILZATION GUIDE

SALES

Global People:

1. Be sure to provide a general overview of your product or service.
2. Skip the details.
3. Avoid sequences in your explanation.
4. Use generalities and simple summaries of your product or service.
5. Know when to be quiet as far as giving too much information.

Specific People:

1. Be sure to present many precise details about your product or service.
2. Describe the details in a logical order.
3. Avoid fluff.
4. Use proper nouns and avoid simple sentences.
5. Be prepared to provide specific objections.

MANAGEMENT

Global People:

1. Explain the task in a general manner, providing a simple overview.
2. Provide global generalities, filling in few details and only when necessary within a global framework.
3. Avoid giving details about what has to be done.
4. Use simple sentences with few modifiers.
5. Macro-manage by emphasizing the forest for the trees.

Specific People:

1. Explain the task with specificity of details.
2. Describe what has to be done in a logical sequence.
3. Avoid using generalizations.
4. Do not expect them to understand or to see the big picture.
5. Micro-manage by emphasizing the trees for the forest.

LANGUAGE TO INFLUENCE

Global People:

Big picture, summary, in general, rundown, framework, large scale, taken as a whole, general idea, overview, largely, synopsis, in the main, by and large, forest for the trees, overall, generally, most of the time, on the whole, as a rule, for the most part, as often as not, generally speaking, all in all.

Specific People:

Precisely, exactly, detailed, precise, in depth, exact, unambiguous, in particular, specifically, definite, meticulous, thoroughly, first, second then next, in detail, in depth, explicit, clear cut, thorough, specific, profoundly, methodical, exhaustive, trees for the forest, above all, comprehensive, all inclusive, defined.

Chapter IX

THE DECISION PEOPLE PATTERN™

Reveals how people really make decisions

Types:

A. Looks Right

B. Sounds Right

C. Feels Right

D. Makes Sense

The **Decision People Pattern™** reveals the way in which we mentally make decisions. This process is usually outside of our conscious awareness. Most of us have little or no awareness of how we make decisions in our lives. In fact, most of us believe that we make decisions because they make sense to us.

The truth of the matter is that very few people, less than 5% of the population, actually makes decisions in this way. Furthermore, some of the dumbest decisions are made based on sense. The reality is that we decide to do things based on one of the four following reasons:

1. It looks right

2. It sounds right

3. It feels right

4. It makes sense

The reason for this is that when something *looks right, sounds right* or *feels right*, it makes sense to us. Yet sense to one person does not translate into sense for another person. We have been programmed in society to believe that what we do *"makes sense."* Most people are totally unaware of the limitations of *"makes sense."* In general, sense means presenting a deductive argument that is based on certain premises that lead to a particular conclusion.

In reality, when things look right, sound right or feel right in our minds, they seem to make sense to us. And, although they make sense to us, it is not in the realm of logic or logical reasoning. In short, then, we most often make decisions based on **looks right, sounds right** or **feels right**. Because of our human need to justify decisions to ourselves or to others, whether to our spouses, friends, or business associates, we then attempt to make sense of the sensory representation that we create in our minds. That is why we often tell ourselves or hear others say, "That makes sense." This response is simply the expression of an internal sensation created when our **Looks Right, Sounds Right** or **Feels Right, Decision People Pattern™** is confirmed.

The whole decision making process involves a specific formula to which we refer as a *strategy,* and which is composed of several parts. In this introductory book, we are simply focusing on the four essence elements of the **Decision People Pattern™**. Let us now consider each of these four elements.

DESCRIPTION

LOOKS RIGHT People

Looks Right people do things based on an internal picture that they are making to themselves on their personal mental screen that literally looks right to them.

SOUNDS RIGHT People

Sounds Right people do things based on an internal auditory representation in the form of a sound or a voice in their head that literally sounds right to them.

FEELS RIGHT People

Feels Right people do things based on an internal sensory representation that takes the form of feeling in some part of their body that literally feels right to them.

MAKES SENSE People

Makes Sense people do things based on an internal sensory representation that takes the form of a remembered feeling, which in their minds is translated as "making sense."

POPULATION DISTRIBUTION

Looks Right: 45%

Sounds Right: 5 to 10%%

Feels Right: 40%

Makes Sense: 5%

TARGET INDICATOR QUESTIONS

Why did you do that? (Refer to something specific.)

Why did you make that decision? (Refer to something specific.)

N.B. If you get a general answer, ask for specifics such as, "What were you seeing, hearing or feeling at the time?"

IDENTIFICATION

Looks Right People: = LR

1. Consider the visual aspects of a situation, person, or thing to be most important to them
2. Are attracted to how things look
3. Like to see visual examples of things
4. Thrive on graphic material such as illustrations, videos and diagrams
5. Are highly visual

Sounds Right People: = SR

1. Focus on the auditory component of a situation or person that can take the form of a sound or voice, internal or external to them
2. Are excellent at calibrating voice tonality variation in others
3. Are attracted to pleasant sounds and voices
4. Are offended by and/or annoyed by loud or harsh sounds and voices
5. Are highly auditory

Feels Right People: = FR

1. Focus on the internal feeling that is triggered in a given situation
2. Thrive on doing, moving around and experiencing movement and sensation in their bodies
3. Like making physical contact such as handshakes or taps on the shoulder
4. Like to experience things, to do things and to have a tactile sensation of things.
5. Are highly kinesthetic

Makes Sense People: = MS

1. Thrive in a world of facts and data

2. Tend to have checklists of criteria in making decisions

3. Don't particularly care about how things look, sound or feel

4. Like to have logical reasons for doing things

5. Tend to have monotone voices with little voice variability

EXAMPLES

Why? Because it looks right to me. LR

I decided on that school for my child because when I visited the place it looked good to me. LR

I chose that tie because I liked the way it looked on me and was perfect for the Annual Meeting. LR

Why? Because it sounds right to me. SR

I chose to hire him because he sounded like he was honest and had integrity. SR

I decided to buy the speakers on the spot because the sound quality impressed me. SR

Why? Because it feels right to me. FR

I decided to go with that computer because I had a gut feeling that told me it was the right thing to do. FR

I choose to have Cheryl on the team because she makes people feel comfortable in her presence, including myself. FR

Why? Because it makes sense. MS

I decided to purchase my car because it met a series of specific criteria which I've been considering for several months now. MS

Dealing with the situation this way made sense to me because I had already thought out and written out the logical pros and cons. MS

UTILZATION GUIDE

SALES

Looks Right People:

1. Describe or provide a photograph, slide or movie of your product or service.
2. Invite the client or customer to imagine using your product or service in a way that looks right to them.
3. Let the customer see the product if possible.
4. Tell stories that the customer can visualize.
5. Use visual metaphors and visual language.

Sounds Right People:

1. Get the customer or client into a dialogue (or express to themselves in a way that sounds right to him or to her) about your product or service with them talking about it in a favorable tonality.
2. Be sure to speak to your customer or client in a pleasant tone of voice, avoiding loud, boisterous, disagreeable, or incongruent tonality.
3. Play soft music in the background if possible and vary your voice.
4. If relevant and possible, have the customer or client listen to or "hear" the product working.
5. Use auditory metaphors and auditory language.

Feels Right People:

1. Let your customer or client use your product on the spot, if possible, or else allow him or her to take it and test it for approval.
2. Get them to represent a feeling that feels right to them about your interaction with them.
3. Avoid giving facts and data.
4. Discuss and elicit their good feelings about using your product or service.

5. Shake their hands at the end of the sale and use sensory-based language.

Makes Sense People:

1. Provide sufficient data and facts to back up your product or service.
2. Explain the specific benefits you can provide.
3. Tell them exactly why they should buy from you and give a list of reasons.
4. Avoid feeling based discussions.
5. Use abstract, non-sensory language.

MANAGEMENT

Looks Right People:

1. Show them how to specifically execute the task or get something done.
2. Use diagrams and visual aids when possible.
3. Literally create a picture for them of how to do what they are supposed to be doing.
4. Demonstrate the task involved so they can visually see how it is done.
5. Use visual metaphors and language in your communication.

Sounds Right People:

1. Tell them how to do the job or how to execute the task in a pleasant tone of voice.
2. Have them engage in their own internal voice describing to themselves precisely what they have to do to successfully execute the task or job at hand.
3. Let them hear what others are saying about the positive aspects of the job.
4. Vary your voice and avoid harsh or loud tonality.
5. Use auditory metaphors and language in your communication.

Feels Right People:

1. Have them internally sense and feel what they are supposed to do.
2. Tell appropriate stories to elicit a positive emotional response about the job or task at hand.

3. Allow them extra time (they need it for their feelings) to move them to the desired state.

4. Don't expect them to learn from manuals or to respond to data and reasons for doing the job.

5. Use sensory-based metaphors and language.

Makes Sense People:

1. Provide appropriate data and facts to describe what they are to do.

2. Answer all of their "why" questions.

3. Give them specific reasons for what they have to do that literally makes sense to them.

4. Be certain to have manuals and reference material available for their perusal.

5. Use abstract, non-sensory based language.

LANGUAGE TO INFLUENCE

Looks Right People

Envision, see, picture, imagine, visualize, see in your mind's eye, look, photograph, take a look, glance, observe, transparent, radiant, brilliant, sparkling, view, watch, fix your eyes on, stare, appear, take a look, gaze, peer, looks right, perspective, viewpoint, vivid, twinkle, outlook, perception, focus, observation, image, in color, sharp, illustration, illustrate, diagram, at a glance, a brilliant idea; a bird's eye view; mental image, illuminate, mental picture, clear cut, looks great to me, you can clearly see, in light of, shed light on, I see what you are saying, I see what you mean, paint a picture, see eye to eye, it shows that, clear vision, a dazzling opportunity.

Sounds Right People

Speak, tell, listen, say, hear, sounds, loud, soft, call, sounds right, sounds good, wavelength, speech, ring, melody, melodious, accent, that resonates, silent, noisy, announce, have an earful, outspoken, that rings a bell, turn a deaf ear to, on the tip of my tongue, proclaim, reverberate, voice an opinion, broadcast, that idea clicks, decree, language, pronounce, translate, tune into, be on the same wavelength, say it loud and clear, utter a sound, march to the same tune, manner of speaking, to tell the truth, sharp tongued, ring true, musical, pleasant sounding, clearly stated, music to my ears, the power of speech, sing, mouthful, hearing, deaf and dumb, echo, mark my words, dissonant, harmonious, harmonic.

Feels Right People

Feeling, sensation, do experience, touch, hard, soft, flow, hot, cold, warm, smooth, coarse, rough, sticky, sensitive, insensitive, light, heavy, weak, strong, firm, solid, tight, loose, concrete, texture, stroke, feel right, touch base, get a handle on, catch, get a handle on, get in touch with, get the drift of, keep a stiff upper lip, be on solid ground, got to hand it to___, get a grip on, get a load of, come to grips with, to connect with, pull some strings, do you feel what I am saying, be cool, calm and collected, be all washed up, lay a hand on, on the surface, consistency, have a firm grip on, grasp an idea or concept, get a grip, to have hold on someone, tackle a problem, be connected to, hard line, scratch the surface.

Make Sense People

Cogent, rational, logical, logic, fact, data, information, sense, make sense, think, ponder, process, analyze, synthesize, premise, intellectualize, concept, idea, assess, conceptualize, learn, consider, calculate, create, appraise, analytical, brains, understand, comprehend, *raison d'etre*, understanding, reason, comprehension, rationale, proposition, know, knowledge, judgment, formula, documentation, paperwork, intellect, manuals, instructions, gauge, have a sense of, all things considered, summarize, ruminate, make sense of, have a sense of, evaluate, think it over, make an appraisal of, hypothesis, recognize, summary, review, reflect, assume, compute, solve an problem, a logical sequence.

EPILOGUE

We hope that you have found this information helpful and that now you can see just how powerful *People Patterns*™ and *Personality Language*™ truly are in your life. While this is just the tip of the iceberg as it were, you now have a good foundation and framework to build upon with your knowledge of what true human interaction is about. *People Patterns*™ that make up our respective *Personality Language*™ go beyond gender differences and differences of race, nationality, and religion.

In reading this book, you have gained powerful insights into human behavior. Furthermore, you now have a unique perspective into the foundation of human communication. In adopting and using the knowledge you have acquired, you now have a decided edge in both your business and in your personal relationships. Among other things, you will begin to make better decisions. You will increase your sales. You will become a much more effective manager, a more effective negotiator and more. You will know how to motivate yourself and others. You will enhance your overall interactions with those you know as well as with people you meet for the first time.

You now have a better understanding of why people act and react the way they do in different situations, including even yourself. It may seem like a lot of information and it is. You will find, however, that in the days and weeks ahead, you will be having "aha" moments. At these times, you will realize why certain interactions you have had with people simply did not work the way you had expected or else they may not have turned out the way in which you would have liked. The light bulb will go off and you'll wonder why you didn't have this *Personality Language*™ information before. It would have made life a lot easier in many ways.

We remind you to use this information wisely and with integrity. In fact, we expect you to do so. We invite you to use *People Patterns*™ and *Personality Language*™ to build bridges of understanding rather than discord, to open doors to prosperity rather than to scarcity, and to create paths of personal growth rather than mindless vegetation.

Finally, we expect you to honor the pledge that you took at the beginning of this book. Not to do so, is to dishonor both yourself and all those who cross your path, as well as the rest of humankind.

Remember that with power comes great responsibility.

APPENDIX

Further Information about the Use of *People Patterns* ™ and *Personality Language* ™

If you are interested in finding out additional information that delves more deeply into *People Patterns*™ and *Personality Language*™, and which will provide you with a refined understanding, then you have come to the right place.

We will be releasing a whole Library examining *Personality Language*™ in different contexts and situations. We know that you are probably busier than ever, and want to gain access to easily understandable, and most importantly, readily usable information, so we have designed our *Personality Language*™ Library components to be mixed and matched to fit your needs. The components are concise, informative, user-friendly and implementable; and they are affordable as well..

Here is just a taste of what will soon be available to you:

Personality Language™ **For Salespeople** – How to *use Personality Language*™ to increase sales dramatically.

Personality Language™ **For Managers** – We will show you as a manager how to use *Personality Language*™ to easily and effectively manage your staff and get more done is less time than you ever thought possible.

Personality Language™ **For Entrepreneurs** – If you would like to know how to refine your skills as an Entrepreneur and take them to the next level of success and beyond, then this will reveal exactly how.

Personality Language™ **For Relationships** – If you have ever wondered how you can choose the person with whom you have the best chance of having a successful relationship, then you need to do yourself a favor and get this part of our Library. It will make having a bad date a thing of the past and you can finally find a person with whom you can have a good chance of being compatible on a long term basis. Plus, you can use this to get a good idea of compatibility in just one conversation, even if it only lasts for 5 minutes.

***Personality Language*™ For Parents** – This is a must for all parents. Find out what makes your child tick and learn how you can finally communicate with your child or children in a fashion that is easy and pain free for all involved.

***Personality Language*™ For The CEO** – In this competitive economic climate in which we live, the successful CEO needs all of the effective tools that one can have at one's disposal and to make sure that one has the right managers in the right positions. We will show you how to do exactly that and more. You will find out how you can use our *Personality Language*™ throughout your organization to increase efficiency, and most importantly your bottom line.

We also have a series of behavioral assessments tools available for use in a corporate setting as well as for small groups. We created these customized instruments to identify specific patterns that we, as behavioral modelers and experts in human typologies, have found to be task specific to increase performance and productivity. For example, for personnel and hiring, we have developed our *Profiling Plus*™ *Profile* to hone in on traits which enhance productivity and success with particular jobs (also a predictive behaviors indicator). Our "*Value Culture*™ *Profile*" predicts future performance of employees and organizations. It also identifies the dynamics of any given corporate entity or organization and the changes needed to increase performance and productivity levels. We have many other assessment tools to fit different contexts of the work environment. For more information, contact us at: info@PersonalityLanguage.com.

As professional behavioral modelers, we have synthesized a great deal of information about human expertise, behavioral change, how people learn and what it takes to achieve elite performance in a variety of domains. As such, we have developed a variety of workshops and programs that we provide as in-house trainings for corporations, including Elite Sales Trainings, Elite Negotiations, Time Management, Stress Management, Learning How to Learn™ Technology, Interpersonal Dynamics, Creativity, Dealing with Change, Strategic Planning, Trainers Trainings, and many more.

APPENDIX

We also provide a corporate package that includes business management consulting services, customized *People Pattern*™ templates to fit your specific needs and integration of our typologies to increase your profitability and enhance your customer relations in every aspect of your business. We also provide in-house trainings on *People Patterns*™ and Personality Language™ for sales teams, for management, for supervisors and much more. For specific information about our various trainings and business consulting and coaching services, contact us at: info@PersonalityLanguage.com.

Much more is on the way! Stay tuned...

Thank you!

Marilyne Woodsmall and Wyatt Woodsmall

ABOUT THE AUTHORS

Marilyne Woodsmall, Ph.M., and Wyatt Woodsmall, Ph.D., are renowned behavioral modelers, international trainers, and experts in human typological research. For over two decades they have synthesized their expertise and research in the areas of performance enhancement, entrepreneurship, learning and creativity, communication, leadership, management science, Neuro-Linguistic Programming (NLP), and cultural change.

Known as the *experts on experts™*, they are the principals of *Advanced Behavioral Modeling™*, Inc., a consulting and training firm committed to increasing the performance and productivity of organizations and individuals using advanced behavioral science and learning technologies. They co-created *Advanced Behavioral Modeling™ Technology,* a behavioral science change technology for capturing, explicating, replicating and transferring expertise. They have pioneered its development and application in numerous fields and have designed model-based trainings to increase and maintain high performance levels in high stress situations in private and corporate sectors and in athletic competition. The result: dramatically increased performance, reduced training time and slashed costs.

They have worked with Fortune 100 companies, governments, top executives and managers, cutting-edge health care researchers, pioneering educators, as well as world class athletes including Olympic Medalists and Olympic Coaches.

The Woodsmalls are also experts in human typologies and created the *International Research Institute for Human Typological Studies*, specializing in research on human difference. They emphasize the connection between human differences and performance and the shaping of cultures to create high performance organizations and global cooperation. They design and implement organizational and culture-shaping projects to strengthen the productivity of people and technology, integrating socio-technical values models to enhance productivity in a world where the interconnectedness of people and technology demand innovative approaches to deal with change.

PERSONALITY LANGUAGE™

These highly respected international trainers and business consultants conduct trainings on five continents, including entrepreneurship, creativity, learning, leadership, values, culture-shaping, stress and time management, sales, negotiations, coaching, *People Patterns*™ and *Personality Language*™, and performance enhancement, and have conducted 38 nineteen day NLP Trainer's Trainings.

In the late eighties the Woodsmalls created *Learning How to Learn Technology*™, focusing on how people learn. Their trainings and workshops are part of *The CLWF Institute for Global Leadership,* created by Marilyne Woodsmall (www.theclwf.org), whose mission is to develop enlightened global leaders and entrepreneurs capable of critical and creative thinking, using new educational models and innovative technologies from different fields. For information, contact info@theclwf.org.

For more information about visit: www.ScienceOfidiots.com. As a purchaser of this book you can also get a FREE 14 Day Pass for our Silver Membership Program. The varied Programs can help you integrate *Personality Language*™ into your business. To learn more about their trainings, CDs and other products, visit:

www.peoplepatternpower.com
www.thefutureoflearning.com
www.themichelthomasmethod.com
www.personalitylanguage.com
www.scienceofidiots.com
www.mindbraintechnologies.com
www.newmindsforthefuture.com
www.thechildrenoflightandwisdomfoundation.org

Made in the USA
Charleston, SC
17 December 2009